D0178427

Printing

Sue Nicholson

QED Publishing

Copyright © QED Publishing 2005

First published in the UK in 2005 by
QED Publishing
A Quarto Group company
226 City Road
London EC1V 2TT

www.qed-publishing.com

A Catalogue record for this book is available from the British Library.

ISBN 1 84538 417 2

Written by Sue Nicholson
Designed by Susi Martin
Photographer Michael Wicks
Editor Paul Manning

Publisher Steve Evans
Creative Director Louise Morley
Editorial Manager Jean Coppendale

The author and publisher would like to thank Millie and Emily, and Sarah Morley for making the models.

Printed and bound in ...

Note to teachers and parents

The projects in this book are aimed at children at Key Stage 1 and are presented in order of difficulty – from easy to more challenging. Each can be used as a stand-alone activity or as part of another area of study.

While the ideas here are offered as inspiration, children should always be encouraged to work from their imagination and first-hand observation.

All projects in this book require adult supervision.

Sourcing ideas

★ Encourage children to source ideas from their own experiences, as well as from books, magazines, the Internet, galleries or museums.
★ Prompt them to talk about different types of art that they have seen at home or on holiday.

★ Use the 'Click for Art!' boxes as a starting point for finding useful material on the Internet.*
★ Suggest that each child keeps a sketchbook of their ideas and their favourite prints.

Evaluating work

★ Encourage children to share and compare their work with others. What do they like best/least about it? If they did the project again, what would they do differently?
★ Help children to judge the originality of their work and to appreciate the different qualities in others' work. This will help them to value ways of working that are different from their own.
★ Encourage children by displaying their work.

* Website information is correct at the time of going to press. However, the publishers cannot accept liability for information or links found on third-party websites.

Contents

Getting started	4
Body prints	6
Leaf prints	8
Junk prints	10
Food prints	12
Block prints	14
String prints	16
Stencil prints	18
One-off prints	20
Marbling	22
Glossary	24
Index	24

Words in bold, **like this**, are explained in the Glossary on page 24.

Getting started

This book will show you how to make fantastic prints from cardboard, sponges, leaves – even food.
Here are some of the things you will need:

Basic equipment

- Paper and card
- Poster/**acrylic** paints
- Pencils and paintbrushes
- Safety scissors
- **PVA glue** or other white glue
- Ruler

You will also need some extra items which are listed separately for each project.

Paper

You can make prints on white paper, coloured paper or cardboard.

Printing blocks

You can make your own **printing blocks** from craft foam, sponges or card cut into different shapes.

Paints for printing

The best paints to use are poster paints or acrylic paints. Use fabric paints for printing on cloth.

Don't forget to spread some newspaper to work on, and to wear an apron to keep your clothes clean.

Take care!

Some projects involve cutting, ironing and photocopying. Always ask an adult for help where you see this sign:

Bits and bobs

Keep a big box full of things you can use to make prints. Look out for items with an interesting **texture** or shape. For example:

★ the end of a thick piece of cardboard
★ an old sponge or cork
★ a piece of knitted wool
★ bubble wrap
★ a Lego® brick
★ a feather

Brushes and paint dishes

You will need different-sized paintbrushes and some saucers or dishes for your paints.

A **printing roller** is also useful for spreading paint evenly on a flat surface.

Body prints

You can make fantastic prints with your hands or fingertips! Just follow these easy steps.

Top tip
Keep a bowl of soapy water and a towel handy. Clean your fingers before you dip them in a new colour.

Butterfly frieze

1 Paint green grass and blue sky on a large sheet of paper and leave it to dry.

You will need:
- A large sheet of white paper
- Thin white card
- Felt-tip pen or pipe cleaners

2 Ask an adult to help you photocopy and cut out butterfly shapes like this from thin white card.

Apple prints

1 Paint your palm with red paint and press it onto paper.

2 Make a brown stalk by printing with the side of a short piece of card.

3 Press your thumb into green paint to print leaves.

3 Dip your fingertips in paint and press them onto the cut out butterfly shapes.

4 Glue the shapes onto the background. Draw feelers with a felt-tip pen, or glue on pipe cleaners.

Use your fingertips to print these fun animals, then add details with a felt-tip pen.

Click for Art!

To see ancient handprints on cave walls in Australia, go to
www.dvc.vic.gov.au/aav/heritage/mini-posters/14RockArt.pdf

Leaf prints

This project shows you how to make
a printed leaf border for a picture or poem.

1 To make the border,
draw a straight line
6cm in from each side
of your sheet of sugar
paper or card. Ask an
adult to cut out the
middle section for you.

2 Paint the underside
of a leaf and press it
onto the frame in
one corner.

3 Use the same leaf
to make prints in the
other corners. Coat the
leaf with fresh paint
each time.

You will need:
- A selection of
  clean, dry fallen
  leaves
- Coloured **sugar
  paper** or card
  25 x 30cm

4 Build up a **pattern**
of leaf shapes in
different colours all
around the frame.
Try beech, sycamore
and oak leaves.

Click for Art!

To see leaf designs by William Morris, visit **www.morrissociety.org** Click on the designs and follow the links.

Top tips

- Make a test print on scrap paper first.
- Leave one colour to dry before you add the next.

flowers printed from a real flower head

When your border is dry, glue your picture or poem behind it, or use it as a photo frame.

Nature prints

Try making prints with:
- ★ twigs and bark
- ★ flowers
- ★ the underside of a mushroom

stems printed from twigs

Junk prints

Racy rocket

Bits of junk such as scrap card, nails, screws or cotton reels make great prints. But always ask before you use them!

Here are some things to try:

★ **Corrugated** cardboard
★ An empty toilet-roll tube
★ A scrunched-up paper bag
★ Nails, screws or washers
★ An old sponge or cork
★ A Lego® brick or jigsaw piece

screw heads
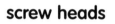

How to make a printing pad

Printing pads use less paint and make a clearer, cleaner print.

Top tip
Don't forget that you will need to make a separate pad for each colour.

1 Ask an adult to help you cut a piece of foam to fit in the bottom of a plastic carton. The easiest way is to place the carton on top of the foam and draw round it first.

2 Pour enough paint into the carton to cover the bottom. Leave it until the foam soaks up the paint.

Stomping robot

plastic bottle top

Build up your picture from bits of junk. Try printing the junk on scrap paper first to see how it looks.

corrugated
cardboard

cork

bubble wrap

Lego® brick

3 Press your bit of junk onto the foam, then press it onto a sheet of paper to make your print.

11

Food prints

Print with fruit or vegetables onto fabric to make fun placemats. Ask an adult to help you with cutting and slicing your food.

Food shapes and patterns

Look for food with interesting patterns or shapes:

★ Dried pasta shapes, such as wheels, long tubes or butterflies

★ A piece of broccoli or cauliflower

★ Half an apple or orange

★ A large cabbage leaf

★ A slice of carrot or celery

★ Half a pepper

1 Set out the foods you are going to print with and some dishes of fabric paint. Work out your design on paper first.

2 Ask an adult to help you cut the calico for the placemats into rectangles 30 x 25cm. Use pinking shears so the edges of the cloth do not fray.

Fabric paints

- Be sure to let each colour dry before you add an overlapping one.
- Most fabric paints need pressing with a hot iron to stop the colours washing out. Ask an adult to do this for you.

Click for Art!

To learn all about traditional block printing on fabric in India, go to **www.sashaworld.com/block/block.htm**

Top tip

Wipe the cut surface of fruit or vegetables dry before you paint it. This helps the paint to stick and you will make a better print.

3 Dip the food into the paint, or paint the surface of the food with a brush. Press down firmly on the cloth to make the print.

13

Block prints

You can make a printing block by gluing a foam shape to a thick piece of card or small block of wood. Printing blocks can be used over and over again.

You will need:
- Craft foam
- Wood, thick card or an empty matchbox for the block

1 Draw a simple shape on a piece of craft foam and ask an adult to help you cut it out.

Top tip
If you want to overlap colours, let one colour dry before you print the next.

2 Glue the foam shape to a small block of wood, an empty matchbox or layers of thick card stuck together.

3 With a brush, paint the shape with poster or acrylic paint.

4 Press the shape onto paper to make a **repeat pattern**.

A simple repeat pattern using one block

A repeat pattern using two blocks

An overlapped pattern using two blocks

Click for Art!
To see Japanese woodblock prints, go to **www.cjn.or.jp/ukiyo-e/arts-index.html** To see a woodcut from Aesop's *Fables*, go to **www.wolmanprints.com/pages/single/all/b/404344.html**

String prints

Make simple printing blocks by gluing string to small pieces of wood or card. The results are stunning!

You will need:
- A piece of wood, thick card, large empty matchbox or a piece of polystyrene for the block
- String

1 Paint a blue watery background onto a sheet of paper or card.

2 When the paint is dry, print tall green reeds with the edge of a long piece of cardboard.

Top tip

Sprinkle a little salt onto the blue paint while wet. This will give the background an interesting grainy texture.

3 Glue string to the printing block in a fish shape. Make a large fish block and a smaller one.

4 Glue on string for the fish's scales. Make an eye from string glued in a spiral or a circle of foam.

5 Paint the printing block and press onto the background. Cover the block with a coat of fresh paint each time you print.

Simple blocks

You can glue all sorts of things to wood or card to make printing blocks:
* ★ Grains of rice
* ★ Nails, screws or washers
* ★ Buttons
* ★ A feather
* ★ Paperclips
* ★ An old key

Print fish swimming in the same direction like real fish.

Print reeds behind and on top of the fish, so the fish appear to be swimming through them.

Stencil prints

Cards decorated with **stencils** are easy to make – and fun to send to your friends!

You will need:
- Thin card for the stencil
- Thick coloured card
- A thick bristly paintbrush

1 Choose a shape that is **symmetrical** – the same on both sides.

2 Fold a sheet of thin card in half. Draw half of the design down the fold.

3 Carefully cut out your stencil and open it out.

4 Fold an A4 sheet of thick coloured card in half lengthwise.

5 Hold your stencil firmly over the front of the card and dab paint through the holes with a thick bristly brush.

Top tip
Use a little paint at a time so it does not leak under the stencil.

Wrapping paper and gift tags

Print stencils in a regular pattern onto plain paper to make a sheet of wrapping paper.

Print a stencil on a square of thick card and hole-punch to make a matching gift tag.

Click for Art!

To see stencils by Yoshitoshi Mori, go to **www.castlefinearts.com/catalog.aspx?catID=97**

19

One-off prints

A **monotype** is a one-off print made by pressing a sheet of paper over a painted picture or design.

You will need:

- A smooth flat surface, such as a desk or a mirror
- A wide paintbrush or a printing roller
- An old comb or a comb made from cardboard
- A pencil or cotton bud

Scraper prints

1 Using a brush or a printing roller, cover a flat surface thickly with paint.

2 Make a pattern in the paint with a pencil or cotton bud, or drag a cardboard comb across the surface.

Stencil monotype

This one-off print of a boat at sea was made by rolling paint over cut-out shapes. A cardboard comb was then dragged through the paint to make the waves.

Top tip

Instead of a desk or mirror, work on a sheet of thick polythene. Tape the sides down with masking tape so it does not move.

Click for Art!

To see **monotype** prints, go to **www.artlex.com** Click on '-Mz page', scroll down to 'monotype', then click on the print titles.

3 While the paint is still wet, press a clean sheet of paper onto your design. Smooth the paper down with your hands or use a clean printing roller.

4 Gently lift up the paper and be careful not to smudge your picture. Leave it on a flat surface to dry.

21

Marbling

In marbling, a beautiful print is made from swirling oil paint dripped into water. Oil and water don't mix, so the oil paint stays on the surface and sticks to the paper.

You will need:
- A large shallow bowl or tray (such as an old washing-up bowl or a baking tin)
- Oil paints and **white spirit**
- Pencil, stick or straw
- Cartridge or other stiff white paper

1 Fill your bowl or tray almost to the top with water.

2 With an adult mix the oil paint with white spirit until the paint is runny.

22

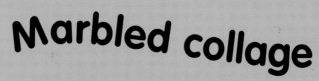

Top tip

When marbling, use just two colours to start with. If you use too many, they will mix together and become muddy.

Cut shapes of marbled paper and stick them onto a background of different-coloured paper so the pictures stand out.

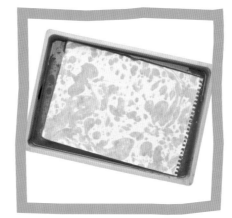

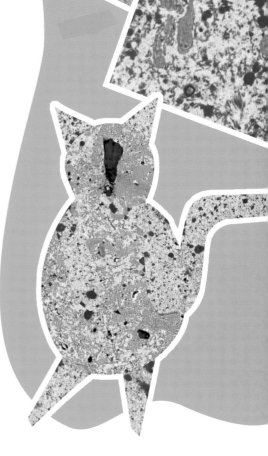

3 Drop tiny blobs of paint onto the water's surface and gently swirl the colours around with a pencil or a stick.

4 Lay your paper on the water's surface. Make sure there are no air bubbles trapped underneath.

Top tip

Instead of stirring the paint with a pencil, try blowing it around the bowl through a straw.

5 Leave for a few seconds, then gently remove the paper. Place the marbled paper on a flat surface to dry.

Click for Art! To see beautiful examples of marbled paper, go to **http://members.aol.com/marbling/marbling** Click on '28 Examples of marbling'.

Glossary

acrylic   easy-to-mix paint that can be cleaned with soap and water

corrugated   type of cardboard with a pattern of ridges and grooves

monotype   one-off print made by pressing a sheet of paper over a painted picture or design

pattern   repetition of shape, line or colour in a design

printing block   object to which paint is applied to make a print

printing roller   tool used to spread paint or ink evenly over the surface to be decorated such as paper

PVA glue   strong white glue that does not wash away

repeat pattern   pattern that has the same shapes, lines or colours used over and over again

stencil   shape cut out of thin card which you can paint or print through

sugar paper   thick, textured paper often used in scrapbooks

symmetrical   shape that is the same on both sides

texture   surface or 'feel' of something

white spirit   liquid used to make oil-based paint more runny

Index

acrylic paints 5, 24
apple prints 7

block prints 14–15
body prints 6–7
brushes 5
butterfly frieze 6–7

collage 23
corrugated cardboard 10, 24

equipment 4–5

fabric paints 5, 12
fingerprints 6–7
foam 10, 11, 14

food prints 12–13

gift tags 19

handprints 6, 7

junk prints 10–11

leaf prints 8–9

marbling 22–23
monotype 20–21, 24

nature prints 9

oil paints 22
one–off prints 20–21

paint dishes 5
paints 5, 12, 22
paper 4, 8
pattern 8, 15, 24

poster paints 5
printing blocks 4, 14–15, 16, 17, 24
printing pads 10–11
printing roller 5, 20, 24
PVA glue 4, 24

racy rocket 10–11

scraper prints 20–21
stencils 18–19, 20, 24
stomping robot 11
string prints 16–17
sugar paper 8, 24

test prints 9, 11
texture 5, 16, 24

white spirit 22, 24
wrapping paper 19